VISIONS
OF MY HEAD THAT
TROUBLES ME

BY: AUTHOR AND WRITER
Mr. Gregory Blue

To order additional copies of this book, contact:
Xlibris
844-714-8691
www.Xlibris.com
Orders@Xlibris.com

ISBN: Softcover   978-1-6698-2175-5
        EBook   978-1-6698-2174-8

Print information available on the last page

Rev. date: 04/25/2022

Please ask God for knowledge and understanding of the reading in my book. For example, just like Matthew, Luke, and the book of John, all speaks about the same topic, but different versions of experience they had. That's the same thing I'm doing, my book, is my version that I wanted to share with the world!!!

Contents

WARNING: THIS BOOK IS ABOUT VISIONS OF MY HEAD THAT TROUBLES ME. THE BOOK CONTAINS MY BELIEF AS A HEBREW ISRAELITE, AND WHAT I HAVE EXPERIENCE AS A MATURE SAINT. MY BOOK MAY OFFEND MANY!! I JUST WANTED TO SHARE MY STORY WITH THE WORLD.

DEDICATION

MY DAUGHTER Jasmine Blue
MY MOTHER Delores Blue
MY DAUGHTER'S MOTHER LAKSHIA BLUE
WILLIE ANDERSON, BOBBY PONDER, HO-YOUNG CHUNG, GRADY WICKER,
BRENDA GATLIN, EARNIE THOMAS, NORTHEASTERN HIGH SCHOOL, THE
HERNS FAMILY, MRS. MAYWEATHER AND FLOYD MAYWEATHER, STEVE
THOMPSON, FRANCIS THERMOND,NADINE TRAYLOR,LIOYD BLUE III,RITA
BLUE, APRIL BLUE, MR.ARTIST RELFORD, MRS.WINSTON,MRS.CURTIS
AND TO ALL MY FAMILY,FRIENDS AND ENEMYS IF THERE ARE ANY!!!!!

CHARACTERS

Narrator- Mr. Gregory Blue

PREFACE

I WANT TO THANK THE LORD JESUS CHRIST FOR MAKING THIS ALL POSSIBLE. MY BOOK IS A SHORT STORY OF THE VISIONS THAT TROUBLED ME DURING MY LIFE. THIS BOOK IS NOT TO OFFEND ANYONE!!! I WANTED TO SHARE MY VISIONS WITH THE WORLD.

ACKNOWLEDGMENT

R.I.P
PASTOR MARKIM
DELORES BLUE
LIOYD BLUE III
ANNIE RUTH TAYLOR

SPECIAL THANKS TO THE FOLLOWING RESEARCH WEBSITES

https://en.m.wikipedia.org

biblegateway.com

https://www.bibleref.com

https://www.blueletterbible.org

https://biblehub.com

Obey the Ten Commandments BY RABBI MARC GELLMAN HTTPS://
WWW.LATIMES.COM/SOCAL/DAILY-PILOT/OPINION/TN-
DPT-ME-0207-GOD-SQUAD-20150206-STORY.HTML

INTRODUCTION- I read that It was once said that Hebrew Israelites facing bad situations today, can turn to **Jeremiah 29:11** .It reads that it is not a promise to immediately rescue us from hardship or suffering, but rather a promise that God has a plan for our lives and regardless of our current situation, He can work through it to prosper us and give us hope.

Narrator- I had to rely on that reading for many years. I've suffered many things from visions in my life, from things that God has revealed to me since I have been on this earth. A man can get into a lot of trouble in this world for two simple reasons, **1.** Being brown skinned and dark, and **2.** Knowing your worth as a black man on this earth.

Narrator- As I sat in my room, I had no one but God to turn too.
I have absolutely no one if I don't have God in my life. I don't even have a friend, the only friend I have is the lord Jesus Christ.I will feel so sad some days, I feel like I have lost my mind, so I had to ask God to be my friend I knew even at a young age, if I didn't put God in my life, I would not live a long life, I would die at a young age, that's how I felt.

<u>Visions in my head that troubles me</u>

Chapter 1- My 1st vision: The woman in my dream

Narrator- I saw a young woman about 27-30 years old, in purple apparel. I saw Hebrew Israelite people in white linen clothes. I saw her turn to me with a clinched slight smile, I saw 3 thrones Yah on the right, I was in the middle, Yah son was on the left of me. I saw Lev priest walking on water feet not touching, carrying the ark of the covenant back to Jerusalem the same presence in the ark is with me says Yah.

Narrator- I never knew who that woman was, I don't know if it was a open vision? To this day, I still have the same vision but I still do not know who the woman is that I saw that day in my vision.

Narrator- My prayer was why I was in my mother's wound, whoever you are, I appreciate you giving me life and I will say whatever you want me to say as long as you don't put me in a place or time too terrible for me to handle. In the womb I had this vision.

Narrator- Once I woke up, I started to pray: My prayer was whoever you are, I appreciate you giving me life and I will say whatever you want me to say as long as you don't put me in a place or time too terrible for me to handle.

Narrator- The vision came back one more time, this time my vision had the sunlight in its strength, in the background like sunlight like there was a big weeping willow tree, no leaves just branches also in my vision I had. I wondered why it would be a tree in my vision.

Chapter 2: My second vision: Baring good fruits

Narrator-I do remember reading about baring good fruits. I bared temperance, faith, love, joy, long suffering, gentleness, and goodness. What does baring good fruits mean? I read that it means the fruit of the Holy Spirit is a term from the bible that touches on nine attributes of a person, also a community living in one accord with the Holy Spirit.

Narrator- According to Chapter 5 of the Epistle to the Galatians, but the fruit of the Spirit is love, joy, peace, patience, kindness, goodness, faithfulness, gentleness, and self-control.

https://en.m.wikipedia.org biblegateway.comhttps://www.bibleref.com

Narrator: In retrospect I remember being over my grandmother house, I can remember when I didn't bare good fruits, me and my cousins we slept in a cabin that was made out of tin and I don't know why I would shoot birds and doves and killed them with my sling shots.

Narrator: I didn't know why I did that because I was so mean and had a temper, but I didn't know that God was training me. I heard my aunt voice from the other house, I would say it was God, and she said it's something about that boy.

Narrator: My grandmother was very strong limber active.She loved life, her family and especially Buster my grand father her husband.Buster was a very good man, full of power, strength, and firmness. He was quiet but extremely dangerous!!

Narrator- As a young child, I saw him kill a hog with a 22 rifle, with a long shank knife.He shot it in the neck, then he jumped the fence and stabbed the hog repeatedly until the hog lost its strength and dropped dead.

Chapter 3- My 3rd vision: I had a vision when I was in Detroit

Narrator- I saw a vision when I was in Detroit, I had just laid down and closed my eyes. I heard people say hi, we are the Hollywood stars and we know that you are one of the greatest Hebrew warriors of this time. We will always love you, then I heard a sound of a cat yell!!

Narrator- A young man spoke and said high my name is Cheng Hi LEE, I'am the greatest oriental master of my time, but I really admire you, however don't pray for me to go to that place, and the things that I show you in my movies, are the things you need to survive.

Narrator- My vision is actually about future movies, actors, and actress. Ahaiah would place in my life to either get help from me about Ahaiah or help me on this journey.

Narrator-Bruce Lee came to me to be used in his movies to show how men like me, navigate through the matrix schemes, plots, agents, and how to avoid danger assassination attempts etc.

Narrator- However the sad thing is I heard him say do not pray for him to go to that place (heaven).I was hard headed and still prayed for him, and I let it go. He was a great man who endured the shame, only to die 1 year shy of our Lord Yah.

Chapter 4-My 4th vision- My military vision

Narrator- When I was in the navy I saw another vision when I was in peal harbor Hawaii with angels had appeared on a horses back with trumpets and I saw the lord Jesus with long woolly hair and he had a white and red robe on, he also had golden keys with a golden key ring and he said behold I'am he that live and that was once dead and I have the keys of hell and of death.

Narrator- I saw angles of revelation who looked like knights, but up close they looked musketeers, faces and body structured very strong with bold faces Negroid features.

Narrator-Horses were white but somehow when close they looked like silver and gray, but life like and they were silver. They rode in the power and ability with the strength of our God, even the horses when they turned they turned boldly and without fear.

Narrator-They were committed to their assignment dedicated to it not to be distracted nor defeated. Their soul purpose was to obey the voice and command of the almighty Ahahia. I love how he works!!

Chapter 5- My 5th vision: God blessed me better than King David and Abraham

Narrator- God bless me better than king David, in my vision, God told me he will give me faith like Abraham to go to California with me.He knew and wanted to show me,he will bring me out because a force against me when I came out of these trials.

Narrator- So I went to California and I used to always say life liberty and the pursuit of happiness that was on my mind.I slept on the floor in the bathroom in the military. I had on old clothes and also a pea coat. I was with many special forces, the strongest men in the world and playing close also I was in and out of jail because the system and I, didn't see eye to eye. I can remember when I was in jail, everyday I only had bologna sandwiches, from time to time.

Narrator- I visioned, two agents called me over, they tied my hands behind my back. I looked up and prayed that the Lord you know I obey you, break these hand cuffs, in the name of Jesus.

Narrator-I fasted seven days like the Lord said. I look toward heaven, and told the lord to break the razors they had in their hands.They took one out, before it touch my wrist, it broke and so did the other. One agent said we should leave him alone, but they never did.

Narrator- They lied and never left me alone even to this day, God just vindicated me recently and I'm 65 years old I can still do things I could do as a young man.

Narrator- None of my natural forces are abated, but God has blessed me to do the work, he has called for me to do from birth.

Narrator- I had a vision,I looked at the wall I said free who shall free Huey. I didn't know what that meant, but he was also a little black panther, with black panther pride, I didn't know it. Huey was the leader of the apparat. I did not have anything to do with them. I was in a concrete hole praising Yah when I saw this on the wall.

Narrator-I was in there about a week then the almighty spoke and said the president is sending F.B.I. agents to you but fear not I shall deliver you. About the 7th day, I heard two men talking but they were in reach from the distance they voice came from, before they did. An old blanket was near me. The almighty ordered me to cover my face for if I behold them they would destroy me.

Narrator- I did what the almighty ordered me to do, and they came with guns drawn. The young Hebrew Israelite men said they are not playing.I said Lord give me wisdom to get out alive. I said why are you all trying to kill me? all I ever did was help people.

Narrator- One of the agents said we should kill him, but the other one said do you not fear Yah if we kill him? then this whole country would go down for this man is a true prophet of Yah. Then they departed praise Yah for grace.

Chapter 6: My 6th vision: Bad pastors

Narrator- Many Pastors today, not all of them, they do not tell the truth most of them say they have saw God and that God gave the visions to all Hebrew Israelite Prophets and some pastors.

https://www.blueletterbible.org

Narrator- In retrospect I know for a fact, that pastors many of them killed people in churches with communion. Deserving the Lord's body, the wine represents the cleansing of our sins by his blood the bread represents the healing of our body, because his body was broken for our healing. There must be a decerment between the two if not many become sick and die because they do not deserve the Lord's body.

Narrator- 1st Corinthians 11:27 reads whoever eats the bread or drinks the cup of the Lord in a bad manner will be guilty of sinning against the body and blood of the Lord, and Lord knows I don't want to be guilty of sinning against the body and blood of the Lord.

https://biblehub.com

Narrator- Pastors today purposely do not tell people the difference between the two, and Life and death is in the power of the tongue and love is to eat the fruit, but a person sinning against the body is not good for that person.

Narrator- The eating of the bread and the drinking of the wine, must be done in the manner that God would accept.

Narrator- Elijah never was heard of until the Lord God used him. He worked many unbelievable miracles signs and wonders.

Narrator- The prophet Joel said in the last days saith yah I shall pour out my spirit upon all flesh, you young men shall see visions and you old men shall dream dreams. Your sons and daughters shall prophesy.

Narrator- The apostle Paul said if there be prophecies, they shall cease but of these three things: faith, hope and charity the greatest of these is charity. Though a man can prophesy, though a man can understand all mysteries have all faith and wisdom, though he gave his body to be burned and have no charity, it shall prophet him nothing.

Narrator-Money is as a bird, it will fly away if its never connected to yah. Yah truth, looks crazy to the fool but to they that love it, is the well spring and the tree of life.

Narrator- The garden unattended grows wild love, it cultivate it to obtain all good fruits.The understanding heart grows upward towards the son of god.

Chapter 7: MY 7ᵗʰ VISION: My vision My Dad was hard on me

Narrator- When I was a child about 8 years old before the mayflower, my dad sat a book in front of me about slavery. My mother loved me, but at 10 years old she had trouble with my 2 sisters and brother. They were very smart and intelligent, but my siblings were so weak when it came to the worldly things of the devils' temptations. Drugs took my 2 sisters and brother life away, but I feel the system killed them. My father was filled with hateful envy, for I even at a young age, my visions were deep and I always turned to God for help.

Narrator- My dad after some time started coming into my room. Man this was evil but at the time I never knew. My dad made me feel like he hated me. The feeling of feeling like your own dad doesn't like you, is not a good feeling at all. In fact, I still feel some kind of way about me and my dad relationship. He did this because he was a mason, and had to prove to them, he was destroying his family for his credibility, for this root goes back to the West African Slave Trade. One time, a long time ago my dad put me out because I wanted to make my own decisions in life, and that didn't sit well with him. I remember asking my dad could I go inside the house because I was too young to leave, my dad said only to get your things and go.

Narrator- I tried to stay in town and get a job with the police department and go to school. I said I could get a grant, but my dad said no!!! He didn't even want to hear what I had to say. What I said went in one ear and out the other ear. I felt my dad just wanted to control my life. My dad would write things down on paper for me to study and learn about the life and the bible. He would say things like if you don't believe it don't read it put it down. God was with me for if I had done that then without a doubt, I would have been destroyed, but even then God was with me.

Chapter 8: My 8ᵗʰ vision: Slavery

Narrator- I always wanted to know about the history of slavery and what my people went through. The visions I have about those time are terrifying. These are visions in my head that troubles me.

Narrator-I saw a deep dark slave ship. People were in it men and women, crying out for me saying little one little one help us, but all of their voices, you could really hear what they were saying.The people said in one accord as they walked to,me in my vision that day,help us please in this mist of trouble.

Narrator- Even today, slaves are looked at like the following: They were chained and shackled up and taken off to slavery

Narrator- When we (**Hebrew Israelites**) came over here on slave ships, the first thing we experienced (**Hebrew Israelites**) was unusual cruelty of punishment.

Narrator- We were beaten and stripped out of our names, for our names carries authority belonging to us from our ancestors, and a nation's power with unity of strength to fight against the devils work.

Narrator- Being in the flesh, what does that really mean? I had to ask myself do I really know the true meaning of being in the flesh. So I wanted to do some research, I found out that the meaning of being in the flesh means a slave to sin.

Narrator-When I turned 65 I began to be fruitful to the lord Jesus Christ to every word that I speak out of my mouth every prayer for his amazing grace he has visit this world with his amazing and graceful spirit of the anointing of the Holy Ghost.

Narrator- I quote, so God told me not to sit with the ministers, the ones with the big cars and rims, the gold chains, and I can take prosecution but when the breathing big dog starts spitting out ice, it's time to vacate! Meaning I don't follow these prophets. They may be stuck up on material things, and not spiritual things.

Narrator- I can remember sitting in amazement, wondering with expectations what will I vision next?

Narrator- God showed me things that I would read about, or see in my visions. The things I would see, would only build more faith inside of me. I love to quote scriptures out loud to myself when I have that feeling of the Lord on me at that moment or that entire day.

Narrator- I saw the heavens roll back like a scroll in living real life picture. I saw people in long white linen clothes with long wolly afros. I saw a young woman 34-35 year's old standing in the front to my left but she was center.

Narrator- Then she turned her face bold but with a royal smile. She slightly bowed towards me. Then I saw 3 thrones on God on the right, I was in the middle and Christ on the left of me. My throne was purple with arms and trimmed with pure gold.

Narrator- Next I saw the Lev priest in synchronized single file walking on H20, their feet did not touch the water. Yah said they are carrying the ark back to Jerusalem. That is my presense in it says God that same presense is with me. This is the last thing David did before he was King.

Narrator-A prophet is not a false prophet by silver nor gold. Every prophet that confesses Christ come in the flesh of Yah, and if they don't, then they are of the Antichrist spirit.

Chapter 9: My 9th vision: My military vision

Narrator- I was 18 years old, I just had got out of high school. The Vietnam War was going and on the news every day. All I saw was C-40 jets with cargo coming in. A lot of caskets of young men and women not even old enough to experience life, but young enough to unfortunately to die for our country.

Narrator- I started taking care of myself at a young age, so when I turned 10 I never asked anyone for a dime! Getting to my parents, I went to my parents' home, my dad met me at the door. My dad wouldn't even allow me to touch the front steps of the house for he had ex-communicated with me, and for no reason commanded me to leave.

Narrator- I had nowhere to turn but to the military. They had said that the Vietnam War was supposed to be over before June 15 but I was listening on the radio and the news that the new wasn't true.

Narrator- President Nixon said the Vietnam war was over within the next day or so with the Vietnam veterans, but they gave us and that's his defensive in the boot camp and took it back during the fall of Saigon knew fighting a heart attack during that time and a lot of my officers and sergeants fought in vietnam they were my trainers for boot camp.

Narrator- I had a girlfriend in the Army in 1975-1978. Her dad was a LTC, he inspired me to be an officer. I went to college, the University of Maryland. They kicked me out. They classified me as a genius.My teacher left the country. I stayed vowed to Yah, I kept it and by grace I'am here today to tell it. I joined the military not to serve the country, but God, I always put him first.

Narrator- So I went to my friend that I had in the Army in Texas, and he turned his back on me. I went into the Navy, so I wouldn't have to die on the streets.

Narrator- So I thought he was my friend, but come to find out he couldn't help me because he was a traitor, a Judas type. He was false, for none could be a witness without the Holy Ghost for he is the bold true witness the Lord himself.

Narrator-Sometimes the sprit stays on me for weeks, the Joy of learning the word of God and seeing evidence is even more amazement for me.

Narrator- Like for instance, sometimes I have vision of my military days, and how God was right there with me, protecting me with his shield of grace and mercy. The things I saw, the death total, and that could have been me.

Narrator- I can remember what happened in 1975 during the Vietnam War. This marked the end of the Vietnam War, also sometimes called the Second Indochina War or the American War. Also, the North Vietnamese captured Saigon on April 30, accepting the surrender of South Vietnam.

Narrator- A enlisted man can tell a sergeant in or out of uniform what rank he is. The same thing goes for an officer. In combat, a platoon leader is examined physically by a commanding General. His words were, are you alright?

Narrator- Regardless of the response, the officer is impaired mentally the general will say quarantine us. I can remember this slender well-built Caucasian man with short hair, I could tell at least he was in his sixties asked me in an authoritative graceful but military carry way, said you alright man thank God for the veterans recognizing good veterans.

Narrator- I prayed that the right people of higher command would talk to me at 2:30 am in the morning. I noticed a knock on the door twice. A tall slender said are you alright? I said yes sir!! And he walked out. When I was in the Navy,I went in to be a officer. I ate in the officers quaters. The captain voice came over the intercom of the ship and said, I was the sharpest sailor in the world. All hell broke loose!!

Narrator- After that I was an E4. In the navy if you are a E5 and up the high ranking officer comes to you they have to promote you. I did not know that the ship captain did this. I did not understand how, because my rank was low. As a prophet I heard the officers above talking to the captain and the captain said blow his mind another black sheep.

Narrator-I was mad for 3 weeks.I inquired Yah the meaning he said he compaired me to **paapy boington** the commander of the black sheep. This is how I ended up in the VA for 5 years not sick but railroaded, but the admiral could mental eveluate you.

Narrator- A higher ranking navy officer night, one came in plain clothes and asked me the question they use to evavlate you. I passed and where I was placed, lots of veterans died. So far, in the last two days a veteran died by a car accident.

Narrator-I lost a lot of family, friends ECT. but I made a vow like everyone else. To protect the consitution and defend against all enemys forien and domestic.

Chapter 10: My 10th vision: Obeying the Ten Commandments

Narrator- According to my understanding of my Hebrew reading, Ahaiah is the Hebrew translation. The biblical Book of Exodus tells the story of the children of Israel and their liberation from slavery in Egypt. It also talks about how God sends ten plagues (rivers of blood, plagues of frogs.) to the Egyptians, and Moses leads the Israelites to the desert and freedom, where they receive the Ten Commandments.

Narrator- the Ten Commandments is something all humans I think struggle with. According to my bible research reading: the Ten Commandments are the following:

Narrator- 1.   I am the Lord your God. You shall not have strange gods before me. You shall not make to thyself any graven thing; nor the likeness of anything that is in heaven above, or in the earth beneath, nor of those things that are in the waters under the earth. You shall not adore them nor serve them.

2.   You shall not take the name of the Lord your God in vain.
3.   Remember to keep holy the Sabbath day.
4.   Honor your father and your mother.
5.   You shall not kill.
6.   You shall not commit adultery.
7.   You shall not steal.
8.   You shall not bear false witness against your neighbor.
9.   You shall not covet your neighbor's wife.
10. You shall not covet your neighbor's goods.

Narrator- We dont have to live by the law.We are under grace.Ahaia asured us he would fufill the law by his death on thecross. His love fulfills the law which he delivered to the saints by love hangs all the law and the prophets this is the new commandment that we love one another as he has loved us.

Obey the Ten Commandments BY RABBI MARC GELLMAN HTTPS://WWW.LATIMES.COM/SOCAL/DAILY-PILOT/OPINION/TN-DPT-ME-0207-GOD-SQUAD-20150206-STORY.HTML

Chapter 11: My 11th vision: Being a homeless veteran

Narrator-So the US honor guard leaders lie to me to force me into homeless military encounters it was God's will I've been here for 4 months. They lied to export the money.

Narrator- See when you are in the military or the docs, they will lie and promise you 100% compensation, but they let me out with only 10% I had an Honorable discharge and I have no one to turn to for help.

Narrator- I can remember back when I was in a shelter for veterans in Detroit Michigan. The veterans and I, was supposed to be in a safe, structured environment designed to lead us back into society through professional guidance and veteran-to-veteran reinforcement.

Narrator- The shelter was supposed to work in collaboration with a few multitude of human service providers, non-profit organizations and governmental agencies to meet the veteran's needs, like medical, psychological and educational needs.

Narrator- They say, never leave a soldier behind. When I hear that saying, it really gets to me. I feel no one cares about the veterans once they are sent back home. 50 percent of the veterans or more are homeless, out in the cold left for dead. I say this from experience, I myself was a homeless veteran, living in a shelter after coming home fighting for our country.

Narrator- When I was in the homeless shelter, I'm for sure I was poisoned by gas I had evil roommates, I would pray out to God that he would send the right people into my room as roommates.

Narrator- "Leave no man behind" is a military code. It is an official part of the Soldier's Creed taught in basic training. Ahaiah assured Ahaiah loves the poor, orphans, homeless, motherless, fatherless,children abused left in the system, oppressed ect. He said I know thy tribulation I know thy poverty but thou are rich.

Narrator-This was introduced as a resolution urging the U.S. to do "everything possible not to leave any members of the armed forces behind during the draw down of Iraq and Afghanistan.

Narrator- They say, never leave a soldier behind. When I hear that saying, it really gets to me. I feel no one cares about the veterans once they are sent back home. 50 percent of the veterans or more are homeless, out in the cold left for dead. I say this from experience, I myself was a homeless veteran, living in a shelter after coming home fighting for our country.

Narrator- When I was in the homeless shelter, I'm for sure I was poisoned by gas I had evil roommates I would pray out to God that he would send the right people into my room as roommates.

Narrator- "Leave no man behind" is a military code. It is an official part of the Soldier's Creed taught in basic training. This was introduced as a resolution urging the U.S. to do "everything possible not to leave any members of the armed forces behind during the draw down of Iraq and Afghanistan.

Narrator- Homeless veterans-In reality, this is the last thing on their minds and agenda. They say the walls are prison institutions, they call you a bum orientate u for drugs and alcohol. Treat you as though you are one step from jail. Man the last thing on their minds is finding housing.

Narrator- Looks like the want us to only reach up and never get out. The Lord is hated so until the blasmey of his name is common conversation and they don't even care to curse the uncursable Yah of heaven. Man this is a crying out pity and irreversible shame.

Narrator- Some people really do try to help veteran's transition back into society. I met a case manager by the name of Mr. Relford when I was homeless, he really care about helping veterans get back on their feet. I can remember when he help me do something that no one else would, he help me write and publish my first book.

Narrator- Not only did Mr. Relford assist me with fulfilling a dream of becoming an author, we also developed a good friendship. We would always talk about scriptures from the bible, or just encourage one another to continue to do right by the man upstairs, the Lord Jesus Christ.

<u>NO WEAPON FORMED AGAINST ME SHALL PROSPER</u>
<u>-Isaiah 54:17</u>

Chapter: I know the smith that walks on the coals of fire I formed the instruments for the waster to destroy no-weapon formed against me shall prosper every tongue. That rises up against thee in judgement thou shalt condemn this is the heritage of the servants of the Lord and their rightness is of me said the Lord of hosts.

In retrospect as I look back pensively about recent affairs, I recall in open places they literally opened fire up on me full force like basic training. It was real live events happening to me at that time.

I told them Esau can't you see those angels snatching bullets out the air. Then I kept going forward and paid them no mind and God persevered me. No that this is Yah's assignment in my life. It is not of private interpretations but Yah's will from the foundation of the world. My birth-rights promised by Yah he said to King David you should never have a son that should not sit upon the throne of Israel.

Chapter 12: MY 12th VISION: God has always be with me

Narrator- Through ups and downs, he was there!!danger and trouble he was there!! Heart ache with an uncurable wound, he was still there!!and through sickness and dispare, he was still there!!Loss and internal, external pain and great stress there.

Narrator- Many traitors, liars, false pretenders close friends turned opposition there mocked by word let down, trouble, tourment death and depression there.

Narrator- God has heal my incurable wound, pain beyond endurance there. In my distress I called upon the Lord, and he healed me.

Narrator-Yes my Yah, my Lord the love in my life, my life line constant companion awesome friend, lover of my soul peace of my life, mender of broken pieces, friend to my brokeness when they all forsook me, the Lord had took me up and God has always been with me. I'am so glad he hepled repaired, restored and delivered me from all evil!! Praise him, praise Yah!! Yah forever and ever amen!!

Chapter 13: My 13th vision: My testimony

Narrator- Lately, I have been telling my testimony everywhere I go. I said the Lord told me get your mind off all they are trying to do to you for I shall give you my ministry to go everywhere healing all that were sick and oppressed of the devil I did this for over 30 years.

Narrator- God has never spoke to me so clear, like he has recently. The knowledge and understanding I have retained, the visions are making a little more sense to me know. I believe the Holy Spirit has found a place in my body, and I'm a mature saint in Christ now.

Narrator- For instance, I started calling God by another name he is known by, the name Yah. When I studied the bible, I learned that the name was a Hebrew name revealed to Moses in the book of Exodus.

Narrator- After going through trial after trial, even death defying the son of God, came to me and said I'am going to give you the same minestry I had, I want you to go everywhere healing the sick and all they that are oppressed of the devil.

Narrator- So I started helping giving to the poor ect. My testimony last year begin in January, close to the end of the month in 2021. A man was at the bus stop freezing to death, he could hardly breath. So I just brought a coat from a friend veteran of mine.

Narrator- I took off the coat I had and placed it on him. He was so cold he couldn't move nor probably feel the coat but in my heart a life was saved.I also gave him all I had to eat, to Yah be the glory!

Narrator- That was an act of God! There was no way I was going to just let the man freeze to death! And I hope if that was me, someone would have done the same thing for me.

Narrator- I love to help anyone I can, that's just the type of person I 'am. Give to the poor, is something I will do the rest of my life. It's something that God has done, and continues to do every day!

Narrator- I know the man that was at the bus stop freezing, he was thankful for what I had done for him, and I could tell he appreciated what I did too.

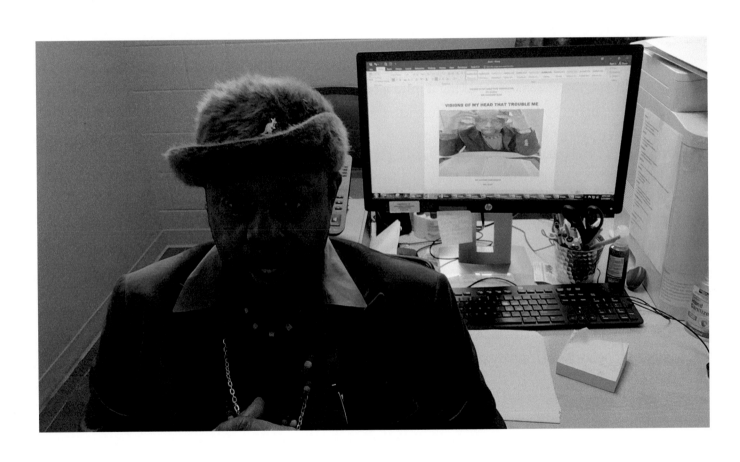

Chapter 14: My vision: I saw a young woman

Narrator- My visions again, while sitting there I saw the heavens above roll back as a living scroll. I saw real people in living color.

Narrator- I saw on my left, Jesus Christ, I was in the middle, God was on the right side, and Israelites with long white clothing. It was a light like the sun that shined.

Narrator- I saw a very young woman by the age of 34 or 35 with a pure crown on her head like a queen would wear.

Narrator- I still want to know. I feel this vision is connect to the Holy Spirit and I feel the Godly Spirit moving throughout out my veins.

Narrator- Next I saw Yah on the right side of me, I was in shock. Then I saw the real Leviticus priest walking barefoot powerfully around in slow motion. I have no clue what this vision means but it was beautiful.

Narartor- I saw a young bronze skinned woman about 34-35 years old. She had a purple gown on with a crown of gold upon her head. She turned towards me, with a goodly but stern anointed look on her face. She bowed slightly this is her abstinence towards me.

Chapter 15: My vision: The Leviticus priest

Narrator- the Leviticus priest was carrying something, but they were walking toward the golden sandy brown water river.

Narrator- I wanted to know what they were carrying, so I prayed for knowledge and understanding, and Yah revealed to me it was the Ark of the Covenant. This was shocking to me. My mind was blown away from what I saw.

Narrator- Their feet never touched the water, it was like they were floating across the water. When my eyes opened, I saw water and sand, again this was a vision in my head that troubles me.The water was some place in Isreal I would say Jordan River.

Narrator- I saw brown skinned men, slender medium built from their thighs down, walking in the spirit and power of almighty Yah. They were in single file. They were carrying the Ark of the Covenant the Lord said after about 7 days of fasting.

Narrator- They were carry back the Ark to Jerusalem and this was the last thing king David did before he was anointed king of Israel. The most high told me also in sequence the same presence in the ark is with me. To yah be the glory.

Chapter 16: MY VISION: I versioned a man with chains

Narrator- This reminds me of the reading and saying: For anyone who speaks in unknown tongues, but they that have the gift to interpret it, does not speak to men but to God. Indeed, no one understands him; he utters mysteries with his spirit, but everyone who prophesies speaks to men for their strengthening, encouragement and comfort. He who speaks in a tongue edifies himself, but he who prophesies edifies the church.

Narrator- I knew I was experiencing speaking in tongues for the longest time, starting at 7 years old. I knew it was the Holy Spirit inside me, my breathing even changed. My heart rate was beating fast, but I had no fear. I wanted to accept the spirit inside my body which is the temple.

Narrator- This reminds me of the reading and saying, In **1 Corinthians 6:19-20** he asks, "Or do you not know that your body is a temple of the Holy Spirit within you, whom you have from God? You are not your own, for you were bought with a price. God created our physical bodies, therefore making it good and precious from the start.

Narrator- These words are deep! I didn't understand how your body could be a temple, but once I retained the information I wanted to start at that moment to start treating my body like a temple. I wanted to start on my mind, body, and soul first. I started to walk in God walk, meaning I stop living for the worldly things, and focus on cleaning my temple, which is my body.

Chapter 17: My vision: Being obedient to God

Narrator- the Lord God has greatly favored me. I glorify his word as a perfect character.

Narrator- 1 John 2:15-17 states do not love the world or the things in the world. If anyone loves the world, the love of the Father is not in him. For all that is in the world, the desires of the flesh and the desires of the eyes and pride in possessions, is not from the Father but is from the world, and the world is passing away along with its desires, but whoever does the will of God abides forever. I love that reading from the bible.

Narrator- Reading that information, makes me want to be obedient to that reading and knowledge. My vision and concern next was the Bible, what does the Bible really mean? And what does each letter stand for in the word Bible? According to research, the english word Bible means the books. As I continue to research, the word itself had the literal meaning of "scroll" and came to be used as the ordinary word for book.

Narrator- When I researched what being obedient to God's walk really meant, I found out that it means, to follow God's commands or requests; also it can mean, to submit to his authority. So this means that I should follow God's commands, as he directed us to do so. For us to have a close relationship with God, we must obey his every command.

Narrator- I always loved the natural environment. Somehow even I myself at a young age, I always wanted to know about where my people came from. I told myself that the next vision I had, I was about 7 and half years old. Why people don't want me to know who I'm? This is why I can't find a house. God is hiding me and wants his servant to dwell in it.

Chapter 18: My vision: I saw KING DAVID

Narrator- This reminds me of the story of King David. I was left astonished from this vision as well. Then I prayed that understanding would be giving to me. King David began his career as an aide. Those actions eventually ensured that he would be "invited" to become king as the true successor of Saul after the latter was slain in battle against the Philistines on Mount Gilboa.

Narrator-The next vision I had, I saw King David in a battle. He was very young about 12-13 years old. He had a sword in his hand, he was so swift and good with the sword, until he hit the blade of the sword on the ground, it never left the ground with the sword, and all I saw was men killed dead on the ground.

Narrator- I remember reading that the Lord sent Nathan to David. The reading said the reason why he came was, when he arrived he spoke there were two men in a certain, I don't know which town, I couldn't see the town in my vision. It was a rich one and the other one was poor. When I continued to read, it said but the poor man had nothing except one small ewe lamb he had bought. The poor man also raised it and it live and grew up with him and his children the reading said. The reading also said it was like a daughter to him, that's how he treated it and loved it.

Narrator- This vision was so clear and felt like a dream. I don't know why my mind is thinking about this vision but I wanted to share it because it has a powerful meaning to it.

Chapter 19: My vision: People look at me funny

Narrator- People look at how I look today and how I dress and speak with intelligence, and have a look of shock on their faces. They can't believe the words that comes out of my mouth that they can research and see they I'm right about a situation or I'm just telling the truth.

Narrator- I guess since my appearance is not like everyone else's is, I'm not supposed to know about life and what I speak on, but whomever looked at me like that, always had a thing coming to them, if they thought I wasn't smart or know what I'm talking about.

Narrator- One thing I will never do, is twist the words of the Lord. I will never be a false prophet, or someone that spread the word incorrectly. I will only believe in one God and one God only, and that's my Lord Jesus Christ.

Narrator- Some people can see and feel the spirit of God is in me, and they accept me like a person, a human being so I stay prayed up every day. This is all I have to turn to, my God!! I remember some of the kids I grew up with, was ashamed to go to church or read the bible. They thought it wasn't cool or you was scared if you went to church, and still to this day, some people say if you scared, then go to church.

Narrator- Well that saying is wrong! I go to church not because I'm scared, but because I'm obedient to my God. Church has helped me a lot. It's my safe heaven and strength to continue own in life and to spread his word to others that may need the Gospel spoken into them. I always enjoy helping someone that can used strength from Gods word. I want them to know how much God loves us all!! No matter black, white, or whatever race you may be, God loves us all.

Narrator- The bible reading of **John 15:12-13**. The reading states the following: "My command is this: Love each other as I have loved you. That saying in itself was enough for me. It was good spiritual food for me. Not only would I speak this out of my mouth to people, I would take them to this scripture to show them what the word states.

Narrator- I can remember this one person ask me, how do I know God loves us? If he loved us, why does all this crime happen? I responded to them with this: the scripture reads this is how the love of God is revealed to us: God has sent his only son into the world so that we can live through him. This is love: it is not that we loved God but that he loved us and God sent his son as the sacrifice that deals with our sins." In spite of these circumstances, I forgive them, and I love them, and give God the glory for they know not what they do.

Narrator- Forgiveness is the greatest act of Yah's love, it brings forth grace. Unmerited favor we do not deserve. Forgiveness is the tool he expressed in victory for no matter what satin or men do, my love prevails through forgiveness. He that forgives, much love to them!

Narrator- We must forgive one another he said until 7 times 70 per day. Satin will constantly bring up things his revolving door of inner sin causing rebellion against the only true friend to men and mankind. He is the one that forgives and cleanses us with his blood, comforts us with his spirit, guides us with his word.

Chapter 20: My vision: I have many talents

Narrator- I have many talents that God blessed me with like for instants, I broke the world record 110 hurdles. I was a high school student 18 years old. I had a modern dance contract. Barry Gordon wanted me in the last dragon. I was one of the youngest black belt martial artist in the city of Detroit at 16 I could have played football for Michigan State University.

Narrator-People was so jealous of me. I did not know it then, but I know it now. Unfortunately no one in my family came to my high school graduation. I had to buy my own clothes starting at 10 years old, I had to pay for my cap and gown pictures myself as a high school kid.

Narrator- I was very hurt coming home by myself, but my coach Mr. Thomas has faith in me, I did not walk by myself, he followed me all the way home desperately calling my name, I could faintly hear him, but somehow, I heard him behind me. I did all I could to dodge him in my mind, I'm at this time 18, and considered a grown man and I had no family support as a grown man.

Narrator- I also saw Samson in my vision, he had bronze skin with powerful strength with powerful muscles, carrying the door post up the hill in his enemy face, on a mission to destroy the adversary of Israel the people of God.

Chapter 21: My vision: Black Hebrew Israelites

Narrator- I wanted to know the true meaning of Black Hebrew Israelites. One time, I researched the meaning, it read that the Black Hebrew Israelites are groups of African Americans who through debut 28 they, are the descendants of the ancient Israelites.

Narrator- From my understanding of the reading, some sub-groups believe that also native and Latin Americans are descendants of the Israelites as well. Israelites were first scattered across the African otherwise known in ancient Mesopotamia.

Narrator- I read the history of when the Israelites were first scattered across the Africa and the whole world. Wow that got my attention quickly. As I continued to read the reading said, The Hebrew Israelite movement is rooted in Israel through Yah and his son from Jacob, Abram, Isaac, a belief system birthed in the by blacks.

Narrator- The reading said they claimed to have received a revelation: America's recently emancipated slaves were God's chosen people, the true Hebrews.

Narrator- According to debut 28, when the Kingdom of Israel was destroyed, the Israelites were first scattered across the entire world continent and then selectively targeted by enemy Esau and enemies of Israel who captured and sold them to European slave traders for bondage in the New World. The research was deep, I wanted to continue.

Narrator- the Hebrew Israelite woman carries the x factor gene. She carries, David, Samson, Gideon, Moses, Samuel etc. Samson was a real Judge anointed by Yah to destroy the Philistines the enemy of Israel. So Esau in our captivity brings up superman, super fly, gangsters, drug dealers etc. To destroy and distort the minds of our youth.

Narrator- Our identity was stolen, our name stripped, family's destroyed, land destroyed, oppressed with an incurable wound that lately in the last few years restored us the yolks of our necks. To help as Satan got scared now the whole world is against us, but Yah will never forget us, he shall show us his undying, unyielding, uncompromising love to his chosen people Israel.

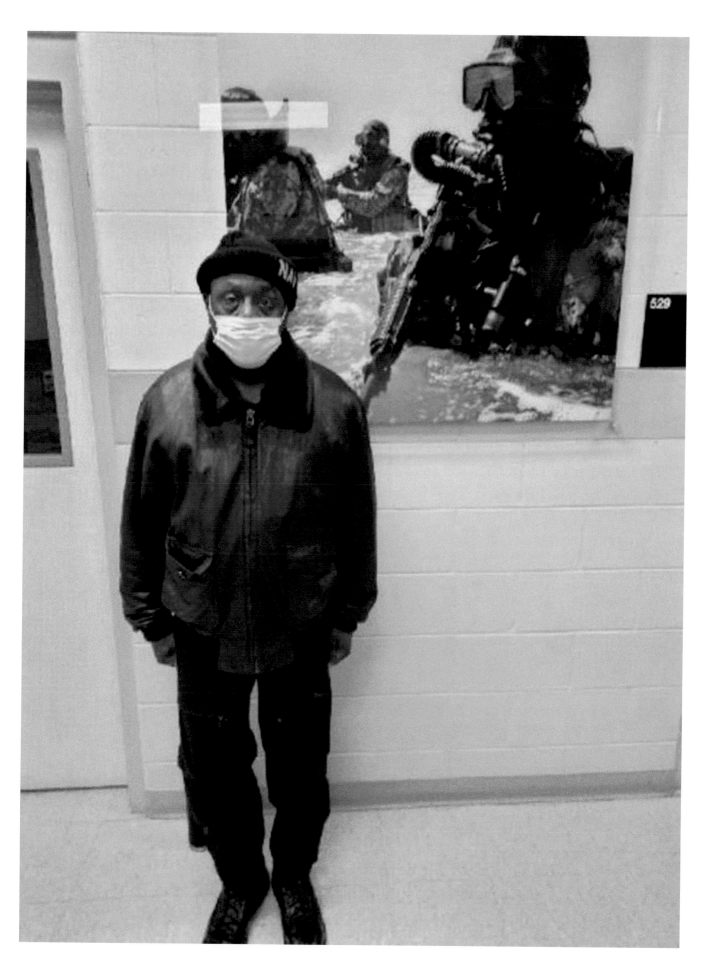

Chapter 22: My vision: Black Judaism

Narrator-Moses was a prophet with the law. All the Old Testament prophets pointed to Jesus Christ. The law has mercy but not grace under the law. All sin was harshly condemned and no one could keep it. If you break one, you break all. When Christ Jesus came on the scene, he brought grace which is unmerited favor. Favor is given that we don't deserve. He once said I come not to destroy the law and the prophets, but to fulfill. He did this on his death on Calvary. When he rose from the dead, the veil of the temple was rent from top to bottom, only Yah had the strength to do this incredible feat.

Shortly after the death of Christ and his ascension to glory, certain religious leaders tried to mix grace with the law. The apostle Paul was a Jew a dark-skinned man of the tribe of Benjamin. Yah used him in a mighty way. In the book of Galatians, Paul stood up against this newfound then but now late religious sect. Judaism is a mixture of law and grace according to the word of Yah. You cannot mix the law and grace together it is unlawful.

BLUE

Narrator-He was like about 8 years old, and in Catholic school that I would tell them don't wish Mary she didn't die for you, Jesus Christ died for you, don't worship that but Jesus died for you because you should put Noah's day before God.

Narrator- It was a secret I said no! I said Yah don't hide nothing! That is a mess for I knew it wasn't Yah.

Narrator- I believed the system tried over and over to poison me. For example, I'm eating in the mess hall, when I was done and I came out, my eyes was blurry. It had to come from the food I was given. I couldn't see anything.

Narrator- Many Angels, wise men disciples and apostles would love to see the day that Yah has blessed me into all my life for the womb to now. Yah is with me even my closest companion my only friend I've been alone all my life. When I was little, a baby pastor from Philadelphia named Elder Jordan told my father I remember hearing them say this is peculiar, tell me she is protected. He did everything the opposite could do to destroy me.

Narrator- A lot of times we get trapped into past present and future dispensation by evil intentions. I want to see the wicked but they're jealous. Again, don't let your left hand know what your right hand is doing, is a quote of that I love to quote.

Narrator- U can get more bees with honey, then vinegar. Don't get bitter, get better! Sermon of the mount expresses Holt life style and Godly living presenting his blessings for it.

Chapter 23: My vision: I made sure I didn't let my left hand know about my right hand.

Narrator- Jesus himself said don't let your left hand know what your right hand is doing, he also said don't let your right hand know what your left hand is doing. He also said, pray now honey where you can get more bees with honey, than vinegar salvation with Christ. Succeed in life as a prophet and you value whole. The devil he don't know what you going to do with you and told you everything I know it's almost look like many people get destroyed, but they should be wise wake up and be assured that the Lord is with thee.

Narrator-I can remember reading about the Sermon on the Mount. Jesus spoke about sharing and giving. I can't remember exactly word for word, but I think it read something like: a person should be aware of learning and practicing the gospel before other people to be seen by those people or person you are preaching in front of, because that person will have no reward from God who is in heaven.

Narrator- I also read that when you give to the needy or a person in need, you are not supposed to let it be known that you help that person in need or brag about what you have done, because that takes way the blessing. God knows what's been done what a person announcing it. The reward comes from the father.

Narrator-This is a good example of the reading I read that states, when you give to the needy or help a person in need, do not let your left hand know what your right hand is doing, so that your giving may be between you that person and Yah, and Yah will reward you. So I don't do good things just too been seen, I do it from the heart!!

Narrator- I get my joy out of seeking someone able to move forward and I was able to assist in some kind of way.

Narrator- My reason for helping others is not for any other reason other than truly helping, just like God would help others. I want to have a good walk, a walk like God, a righteous man. I don't want just a worldly mankind temporary reward, I want an eternal reward from Yah.

Narrator-Another example of not letting your left hand no what your right hand is doing, is to pray in a place by yourself, and do not do it in public. This is done with good from the heart motives.

Narrator-See I have dealt with some people who are concerned toxic people. They are people with bad spirits and unhealthy and can caused problems in your walk with faith and God. When you run into toxic people you can began to feel a certain way, a way that is not normal to you. This is because you have been exposed to a warning that this is not Yah way, and to pray for those who are lose and of toxic.

Narrator- I always felt if I continue my walk and continue to let my light shine, then any toxic people I ran into or have ran into someday they will become better people watching how light just shines on me, and hopefully it rubs off on those individuals.

Narrator- I always wonder about why people would come to church like it was a fashion show. I was raised to come as you are. I can remember this one person telling me that they didn't go to church because they didn't have a suit.

Narrator- To me that was toxic thinking. I told him that God said come as you are!! The guy never heard anyone say that it is ok to go to church in whatever clothes you have. That information change this man life, and the way he feels about going to church.

Narrator- In my experience, the people who come to church and want to make it their business to be seen, are focused on the wrong thing. Yah is behind us to the destiny of my penny pastors prophets saints religious leaders are extremely jealous of me for men has a tendency to take your blessing, and try to take your blessing, and add it to their lifetime dream and be mad because it's not them.

Narrator- well this is just my birth right to be the king of Israel prophecy said to me through the Holy Ghost when I was a baby. Even as a child up into now, it's been 65 years of suffering and going through the years of blessings. We have to believe the ways of Yah over the ways of the enemy even in the land of our enemy.

Chapter 24: My vision: Moses was in my vision

Narrator- Moses the great Levite prophet of Yah once said if there be a prophet among you said yah, I shall speak to him in a vision and he shall dream a dream.

Narrator- In retrospect, the sufferings of the real prophet is the worse of the entire 5 fold ministry. Most prophet's common mental emotional effect is illness, oppression, depression, even some cases suicidal thoughts, brought forth from the enormous pressure from prophesying, reigning or pastoring the entire nation of Israel to carry the staff of almighty Yah to disobedient, dying and stiffed necked folks who defy the arm of the almighty's judgment.

Narrator- When he is worth in fury justice, judgement or destruction is inevitable, and thus the prophet is born when no one wants to hear from Yah. All his life is devoted love for Yah and the deep tearing to share and speak his word. To Yah be the glory saints the prophets of Yah. Let's go higher in him to soar as eagles.

Chapter 25: CLOSING REMARKS
Quotes by: Author: Gregory Blue

-Let determination fuel your fire up to the stars in the sky, for the stars are too low.

-There is a gift, the gift of faith! Yah please grace me to use the faith you have given me.

-Rivers of waters run deep especially to those of strong survival instincts for they don't strive they ultimately survive.

-Fear of Almighty Yah wisdom in persistent state wisdom gained.

-Mastery of one's self, is as a deep pit but he that is of all understanding heart. The dipper of experience shall draw it out.

- All things of Yawashi abound with his faith towards yah.

-Mysteries are for mystical knowledge but the gift of the Holy Ghost shall seek and find it.

-Creativity is the gift of God the color of it is his essence.

-Whenever a man ceased to learn, then death is his next step.

-Pure faith brings comfort, power love, strength and joy in the Holy Ghost.

-Universal force set in the medative mind set helps to bring forth imagery if of Yah then blessed is it.

-Riches and wealth gained through greed swiftly leads to Downward Rivers gushing out sure destruction 4 vexations of lost spirits.

-vanity of all vanity fear without God lost without faith.

-faith in its greatest mountain is where Yah starts to purely examine possible blessings beyond impossibility all things become possible.

-love lost rips the soul breaches the spirit.

-Faith in its fullness Yah in his awesomeness.

-Our sufferings are the Jews of the crown don't manner never complaint only wear it wisely.

-let determination fuel your fire go up for the stars are just too low.

-Interceptive meditatively thinking we have an inner eye if properly used to Yahs glory only it all leashes beauty and perspective building structure to one's positive life love.

-There is a gift the gift of faith yah please grace me to use faith you have given me.

-serve yah through faith through faith truly and love for he returning the gifts in blessings from above approve of yah he does this precious works.

-long life is good but what have we done in the short times.

-even destruction is good when yah is building better.

-whenever a man stops learning he just begins to die.

BIO
Date of Birth- September 2, 1956
Place of Birth- Richmond, Virginia

The book Visions of my head that troubles me, is the life story of an African American writer known as Gregory Blue. This is a story inspired by true events about his life, how he turned to God for every situation he ran across, and growing up with a strict father in the household.

He was born in Richmond, Virginia. He was raised by his mother Deloris Blue and his father Lloyd Blue Jr. His job title in the Military was called Engineer. He was on active duty for 6 years, 3 years in the Army, and 3 years in the Navy. His rank at discharge was E4.

The author Gregory Blue severed in the Army and Navy during the time frame of 06-15-1975-06-15-1981. He had an Honorable discharge but was done wrong once he came home from the Military, and became a homeless veteran.

THE END

Printed in the United States
by Baker & Taylor Publisher Services